MINIBEASTS UP CLOSE

Bees
Up Close

Robin Birch

Raintree

www.raintreepublishers.co.uk
Visit our website to find out more information about **Raintree** books.

To order:
 Phone 44 (0) 1865 888112
 Send a fax to 44 (0) 1865 314091
Visit the Raintree Bookshop at **www.raintreepublishers.co.uk** to browse our catalogue and order online.

Published in 2004 by Heinemann Library
a division of Harcourt Education Australia,
18–22 Salmon Street, Port Melbourne Victoria 3207 Australia
(a division of Reed International Books Australia Pty Ltd,
ABN 70 001 002 357).
Visit the Heinemann Library website @
www.heinemannlibrary.com.au

First published in Great Britain by Raintree,
Halley Court, Jordan Hill, Oxford OX2 8EJ,
part of Harcourt Education.
Raintree is a registered trademark of Harcourt Education Ltd.

A Reed Elsevier company

© Reed International Books Australia Pty Ltd 2004

08 07 06 05 04
10 9 8 7 6 5 4 3 2 1

Editorial: Carmel Heron, Anne McKenna
Design: Stella Vassiliou, Marta White
Photo research: Jes Senbergs, Wendy Duncan
Illustration: Rob Mancini
Production: Tracey Jarrett

Typeset in Officina Sans 19/23 pt
Pre-press by Digital Imaging Group (DIG)
Printed in China by WKT Company Ltd.

The paper used to print this book comes from sustainable resources.

National Library of Australia Cataloguing-in-Publication data:

Birch, Robin.
    Bees up close.

    Includes index.
    For primary students.
    ISBN 1 74070 193 3.

    1. Bees - Juvenile literature. I. Title.
    (Series : Birch, Robin. Minibeasts up close).

595.799

Acknowledgements
The publisher would like to thank the following for permission
to reproduce photographs: ANT Photo Library/Frank Park: p. **7**,
/Otto Rogge: p. **14**; ARDEA London/Pascal Goetgheluck: p. **12**;
Auscape/Anne & Jacques Six: pp. **17, 19, 25**, /Andrew Henley: p. **24**;
Bruce Coleman Inc/Kim Taylor: pp. **8, 20**, /Larry West: p. **16**; Corbis:
pp. **26, 29**; CSIRO: p. **27**; Lochman Transparencies/© Jiri Lochman:
pp. **6, 11**; OSF: pp. **4, 15, 21**; photolibrary.com: pp. **10, 28**; ©
Queensland Museum/Jeff Wright: p. **5**; Science Photo Library/Susumu
Nishinaga: p. **13**, /Gusto: p. **18**.

Cover photograph of worker bee sitting on flower reproduced with
permission of Lochman Transparencies/© Wade Hughes.

Every attempt has been made to trace and acknowledge copyright.
Where an attempt has been unsuccessful, the publisher would be
pleased to hear from the copyright owner so any omission or error
can be rectified.

Contents

Any words appearing in bold, **like this**, are explained in the Glossary.

Amazing bees!

Have you seen bees buzzing around flowers?
Have you wondered what they are doing?
Bees are amazing when you get to know
them, close up.

Bees drink sweet **nectar** from flowers. Then
they turn it into honey, inside them!

Bees spread **pollen** from flower to flower.
Because of this, plants can grow seeds.

Most bees have black and yellow stripes. Some have red or orange stripes and others are green, blue or even red.

What is a bee?

Bees are insects. Insects are animals that have six legs. Insects also have a thin, hard skin called an **exoskeleton** on the outside of the body, instead of bones on the inside of the body.

How many kinds?

There are at least 20,000 different kinds, or **species**, of bees. The biggest bees are about as long as your thumb (4 centimetres). The smallest are about as big as a sesame seed (2 millimetres).

Where do bees live?

Bees live in most parts of the world. They are more often found in warm, wet parts of the world. They do not usually live in very cold places.

Nests under ground

Bees make nests to lay their eggs in. Most kinds of bees make their nests under ground. Many bees live in burrows left behind by rats, mice or termites. Others dig their own burrows.

A bee at the entrance to its underground burrow.

Nests above ground

Some kinds of bees make nests above the ground, on a tree branch or wall. Other bees nest in plant stems, or in old stumps and logs. Some bees nest in hollow tree trunks and in spaces between the walls of buildings.

Honeybee nests

Honeybees make the honey we eat. The shelters that honeybees live in are called **hives**. People make hives for honeybees, so beekeepers can collect the honey.

Bumblebees

Bumblebees often live in cold places such as the United Kingdom. They are one of the biggest bees, and are plump and very hairy.

Bees' nests come in many shapes and sizes.

Bee body parts

A bee's body has three parts. First is the head, then the **thorax** in the middle and then the **abdomen** (<u>ab</u>-da-men) at the end.

The head

On the head are feelers called **antennae** (an-<u>ten</u>-ay), as well as eyes and mouthparts.

head

antenna

eye

abdomen

thorax

wing

The thorax

The thorax has six legs joined to it, three on each side. Bees have two pairs of wings attached to the thorax.

The abdomen

The bee has a very thin waist between the abdomen and thorax. Many bees have a sting right on the end of the abdomen.

The exoskeleton

The bee's **exoskeleton** covers the whole of its body. It gives the bee its shape and protects the bee from being hurt easily. It also stops the bee from drying out by trapping water inside its body. The exoskeleton of most bees is covered with hairs.

Shiny bees

Nomada (no-<u>ma</u>-da) bees do not have many hairs on their exoskeleton. Their exoskeleton is usually bright and shiny.

Mouthparts and eating

Bees eat **nectar** and **pollen**, which are found in flowers.

Making honey

A bee puts its tongue into the middle of a flower and sucks up nectar. The nectar goes into a bag in the bee's body called the honey stomach, where it becomes honey.

Most of the honey comes back out of the bee's mouth later to feed the young and other bees. The bee keeps some honey inside its body for its own food.

tongue

Most bees have a long, thin tongue.

Collecting pollen

Bees use their **jaws** and tongue to bite and scrape pollen from flowers. They carry it back to their nests on hairs on their bodies. They mix it with nectar or honey to make a sticky substance called bee bread. They feed bee bread to their young. Bees only eat a little pollen themselves.

Pollen from a flower sticks to a bee's hairy coat.

Eyes and sensing

A bee has two very large eyes, one on each side of the head. These eyes are made of hundreds of smaller eyes. This kind of eye is called a **compound** eye.

Bees also have three tiny eyes on the top of their head. These eyes most likely only see dark and light. They probably help the bee when it is flying.

A bee can see all around it with its compound eyes.

Finding their way

Bees can work out where they are going by seeing where the sun is in the sky. They use it as a signpost. They also look at trees and other large objects, and use them as signposts too. They are more likely to do this when they have already found food, and are going backwards and forwards from the nest.

Bees have three tiny eyes on top of their head.

Sensing the sun

Bees can see where the sun is, even if it is covered with cloud. This is because they can **sense** the sun through the cloud.

Antennae and sensing

A bee has two long feelers called **antennae** on its head, to **sense** with. They are between the eyes and above the mouth. They can be folded back out of the way if the bee is in danger, or is inside a flower or the nest. This stops them from being damaged.

Smelling

A bee smells with its antennae. The bee keeps going to the same kind of flower as it flies around. It needs to smell the flowers carefully to do this.

Bees' antennae have a bend in them.

Feeling and hearing

A bee touches things with its antennae. It also feels **vibrations** and hears sounds with its antennae. This helps the bee to escape from danger. A bee also feels anything that touches the hairs on its body.

Tasting

A bee has a **palp**, like a finger, on each side of its tongue. There are also two very short palps under the mouth. The bee tastes with its tongue and its palps.

Bees smell and touch flowers with their antennae.

Legs for moving

Bees' legs have three main parts, and a long foot. Bees can walk and run with their legs. They also hold onto flowers with their legs while they are feeding.

The end of the foot has two claws, so the bee can hold onto rough surfaces. There is also a pad with hairs on it at the end of the foot. This gets sticky if the bee needs to walk on something smooth, like a window.

This bumblebee is gripping a blade of grass with its legs, feet and claws.

Useful legs

Many bees have hooks on their legs for pulling **wax** off their **abdomen**, where it is made. Some bees have a hook on their front legs for cleaning their **antennae**.

All bees have hairs on their legs for carrying **pollen**. Many bees have pollen baskets on their back legs. These are wide, flat areas with long hairs around them.

Digging a nest

A digger bee uses its legs to dig its nest in the soil. This kind of bee lives by itself.

← pollen basket

This bee's pollen basket is full of pollen.

17

Wings and flying

Bees fly to find their food, to escape enemies and to start a new nest.

A bee has two pairs of wings. The front wings are larger than the back wings. The wings are clear and very thin. They are held in shape by hard **veins**.

Bees can fly quickly between flowers to find food.

vein

The front and back wings are joined together by a row of tiny hooks. This makes the front and back wings move together, so the bee can fly fast.

Flying

Bees beat their wings very fast, more than 200 times a second. The beating wings make a buzzing sound. Bees can fly forwards, backwards, or hover in one place.

A bee folds its wings back over its body when it is not using them, to protect them.

Clean wings

Bees clean their wings with combs of hair on their back legs.

The thorax and abdomen

A bee's **thorax** has wings and legs joined to it. Strong muscles inside the thorax move the legs and make the wings beat fast.

The **abdomen** is made of sections, which make stripes across it. Many bees have **wax glands** underneath the abdomen. They use wax to make the **cells** in their nests.

A bee's wings and legs are joined to its thorax.

Sting

Many bees have a sting on the end of their abdomen. The bee sticks its sting into an animal, then pumps in a stinging poison. Bees sting animals to teach them to keep away from bees and their nests.

In most bees, the sting has pointed **barbs** that stop the sting from coming out. When the bee moves away, the end of the abdomen is pulled off and the bee dies.

Biting bees

Meliponini (mel-i-pon-<u>ee</u>-nee) bees do not have a sting. If an animal disturbs their nest, they defend themselves by biting, and they crawl into the animal's hair, eyes, ears and nose. Some of them pour burning juice onto the animal.

A bee's sting is a sharp tube on the end of its abdomen.

21

Inside a bee

A bee's heart is long and thin. It runs down the middle of the **abdomen**. It pumps blood around the body.

How do bees get air?

A bee has tiny air holes called **spiracles** (<u>spi</u>-rak-els) down the sides of its **thorax** and abdomen. Air goes in these holes and is carried around the inside of the bee by tiny tubes.

What happens to food?

A bee's honey stomach and food stomach are in its abdomen. Most of the honey in the honey stomach comes back out of the mouth to feed other bees in the nest. If the bee needs some food for itself, honey moves from its honey stomach to its food stomach, for it to **digest**.

Waste passes out of the **anus** (just above the sting) as droppings.

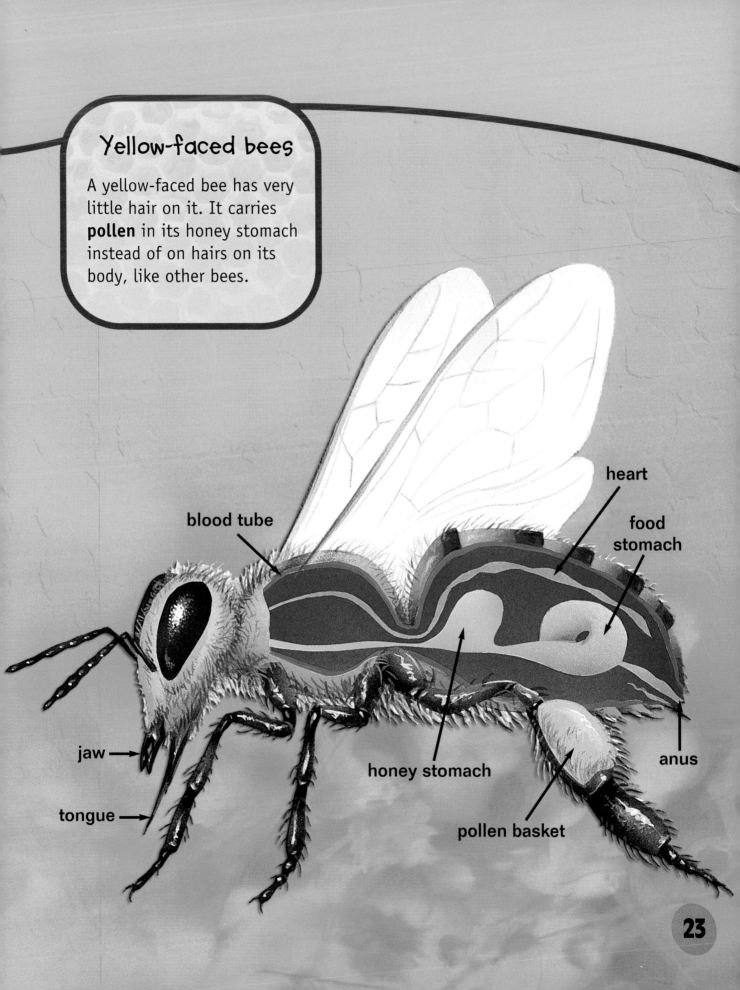

Yellow-faced bees

A yellow-faced bee has very little hair on it. It carries **pollen** in its honey stomach instead of on hairs on its body, like other bees.

blood tube

heart

food stomach

jaw

tongue

honey stomach

pollen basket

anus

23

Living together

Most bees live alone. The females make the nests, usually under ground. Their nests have several **cells** in them, each one for a young bee to grow in. These kinds of bees usually live for a few weeks.

Some bees live in large groups called **colonies**. Their nests have many cells, for many young bees. Honeybees have the largest colonies of all, with thousands of bees in them.

A honeybee's nest is made up of thousands of cells that fit neatly together.

Honeybee colony

There is one queen bee in a honeybee colony. She is a large female, and she lays eggs for the colony. She may live for up to five years.

There are some male bees called drone bees. They do not do any work, and live for four months at the most. They may **mate** with a queen bee.

The worker bees are females that look after the queen, the nest and the young bees. They leave the nest to get food for the colony. They live for a few weeks.

A queen honeybee is surrounded by worker bees.

25

Life cycle of bees

A female bee becomes a mother after she **mates** with a male bee. Bees usually mate while they are flying. The male bee dies soon after.

A mother bee lays her eggs in her nest. One egg goes into each cell in the nest. Then the eggs hatch into **larvae**. The larvae are small grubs, and have no legs.

Growing up

The larvae grow in their cells. In some kinds of bees, the larvae eat food such as honey and **pollen** left for them in their cells. In other kinds, the larvae are fed by the workers.

A mother bee lays an egg in each cell.

After about 6 days, the larvae stop eating and moving, and become **pupae** for about 12 days. This is when they change from larvae into adult bees.

Where does a mother bee go?

In most kinds of bees, the mother bee does not stay in the nest. The young adults also leave the nest. These kinds of bees live alone.

Honeybee queen

In a honeybee **colony**, the mother is called the queen bee. If a young queen bee grows up in the nest, the old one leaves, taking many workers with her to start a new colony. This is called swarming.

In this nest, the worker bees feed the larvae in their cells.

Bees and us

People keep honeybees so they can collect the honey. The honeybees live in **hives**, which are looked after by the beekeeper. The honeybees make rows of **wax cells** in the hive. They fill them with honey, to store for later, for food for themselves and their **larvae**. The beekeeper takes the cells out of the hive and removes some of the honey. The bees are not harmed.

Beekeepers wear protective clothing when they tend bee hives.

Honey is a healthy food.

Bee stings

A bee sting can be very painful. Some people can get sick if they are stung by a bee. When a bee stings you, it leaves its sting behind in the skin. It should be scraped out carefully. If you press it, more poison can go into the skin.

Pollinating crops

Many farmers also keep bees to **pollinate** their **crops**. When there are more bees, more **pollen** can be carried from flower to flower.

Find out for yourself

Try to find some bees visiting flowers. You will probably see more bees on a warm day. Watch as they crawl around on a flower. How long do they stay on each flower? Be careful not to get too close, as you do not want to get stung.

Books to read

Life in a Colony: Bees, Richard and Louise Spilsbury (Heinemann Library, 2004)

Looking at Minibeasts: Ants, Bees and Wasps, Sally Morgan (Belitha Press, 2001)

Using the Internet

Explore the Internet to find out more about bees. Websites can change, so if the links below no longer work, do not worry. Use a search engine, such as www.yahooligans.com or www.internet4kids.com, and type in a keyword such as 'bees', or the name of a particular bee species.

Websites

http://www.pbs.org/wgbh/nova/bees/dances.html
Watch video clips and see images of bees in flight and inside a hive.

http://www.honey.com/kids/index.html
This site has interesting bee facts and trivia, games and yummy honey recipes.

Glossary

abdomen   last of the three main sections of an insect

antenna   (plural: antennae) feeler on an insect's head

anus   hole in the abdomen through which droppings are passed

barb   backward-curving point on the sting

cell   small container, like a small room; each bee larva grows in its own cell

colony   group of many insects of the same kind living together

compound   made of smaller parts

crop   plants grown by farmers

digest   break down food so it can be used for energy and growth

exoskeleton   hard outside skin of an insect

gland   body part that makes something which has a special use, such as wax or a poison

hive   shelter that bees make their nest in

jaw   hard mouthpart used for biting and holding food

larva   (plural: larvae) young stage of many insects, a grub

mate   when a male and a female come together to produce young

nectar   sweet juice inside flowers

palp   small body part like a finger, near an insect's mouth

pollen   substance on flowers made of dry, dusty grains, usually yellow; plants use pollen to reproduce

pollinate   take pollen from one plant to another, so the plants can make seeds

pupa   (plural: pupae) stage of an insect's life, when it changes from a larva to an adult

sense   how an animal knows what is going on around it

species   type or kind of animal; animals of the same species can produce young together

spiracle   tiny air hole on an insect's body, which lets air inside

thorax   chest part of an insect

vein   small tube in the body that carries blood; dry veins in insect wings are empty

vibration   fast shaking movement

wax   firm but soft substance

31

Index